T0032195

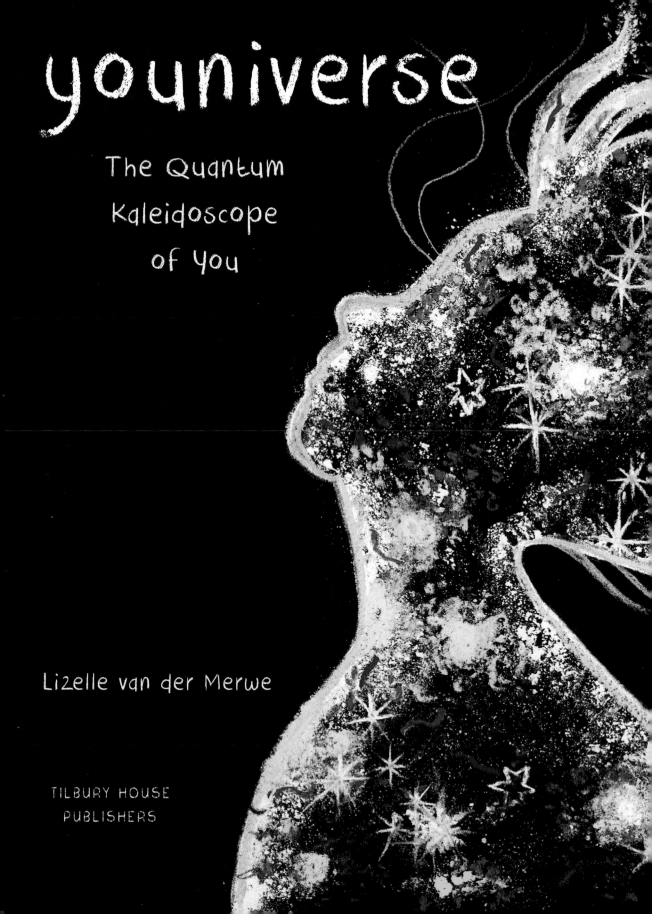

youniverse

The Quantum Kaleidoscope of You

Lizelle van der Merwe

TILBURY HOUSE
PUBLISHERS

"In a sky full of stars
I think I see you
I think I see you."
—Coldplay

This is a story about YOU . . .

. . . about the world you live in,
everything you see and everything
you can't see, all that ever was and
ever will be, the universe around you
and the youniverse that is you.

*A supernova is an
exploding star.*

The universe is infinitely larger
than your youniverse, which
is stupendously larger than
a cell, which is vastly larger
than an atom, which dwarfs
the infinitesimal particles from
which it is made.

This is an electron, a negatively charged particle orbiting the center of an atom, so tiny it can't be measured. A particle is a point in space, but a wave fills space, and an electron is both.

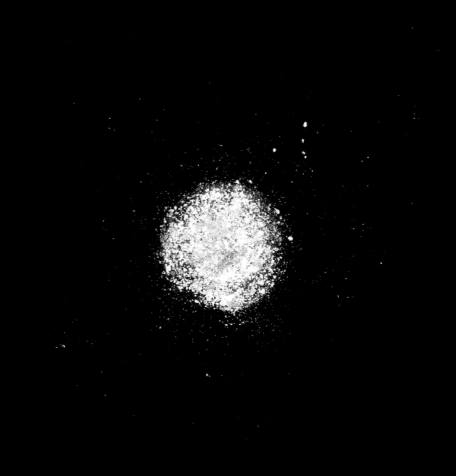

It is like a cloud of fog around the atom's core, and the particle is anywhere in that fog, shaking, vibrating, moving fast.

Electrons are the glue
linking atoms together.
Atoms combine into
molecules by sharing
electrons. That's how they
build your youniverse and
the universe. But when
atoms don't combine,
they push apart.
Press a fingertip
to this page,
and the page
pushes back. The
electron clouds
in the paper push
back against the
electron clouds in
your finger.

Your pressing
distorts the
clouds, and
they resist, or
else your finger
would pass
right through
the book.

Electrons hurl out pulses of light

called photons. Photons are like particles that have no mass, yet they travel as waves of light, so fast they could circle the Earth seven times in one second.

Light bounces from everything you see.

This is an atom. It contains protons and neutrons,
each one impossibly tiny yet more than a thousand
times as heavy as an electron. They bind together
to make the atom's core, or nucleus.

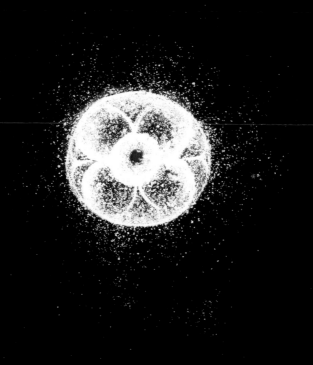

Around it buzzes the cloud of electrons, filling a
space one hundred thousand times larger than
the nucleus yet still almost impossibly small.

Light and atoms weave themselves together . . .

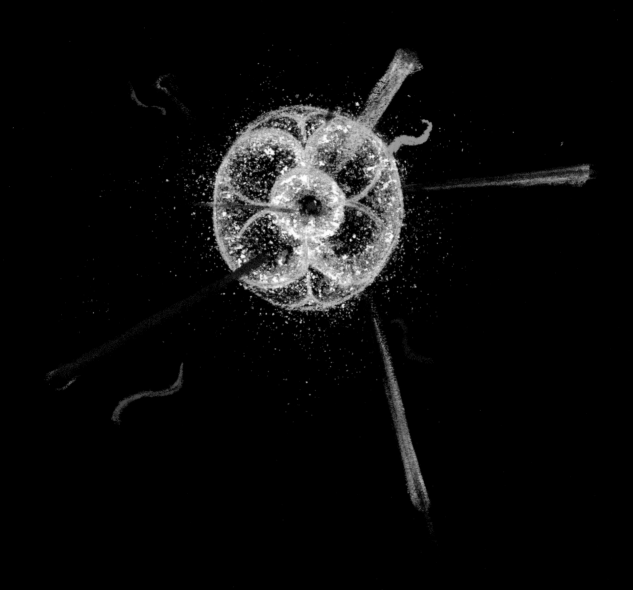

. . . creating the visible kaleidoscope
of your youniverse and the universe.

This is a molecule.

It holds two, three, or even billions of atoms.

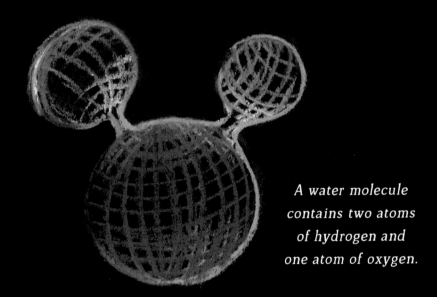

A water molecule contains two atoms of hydrogen and one atom of oxygen.

Molecules are visible under
powerful microscopes, but
they are still very small.

A DNA molecule may
contain 200 billion atoms
of carbon, hydrogen,
oxygen, nitrogen, and
phosphorus, similar to
the number of stars in
the Milky Way galaxy.

This is a blood cell.

It holds many molecules and many, many atoms.

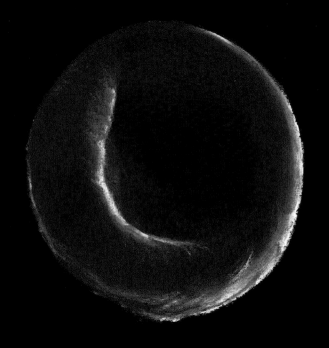

Blood cells flow in rivers through your body, delivering molecules of oxygen to your body's tissues.

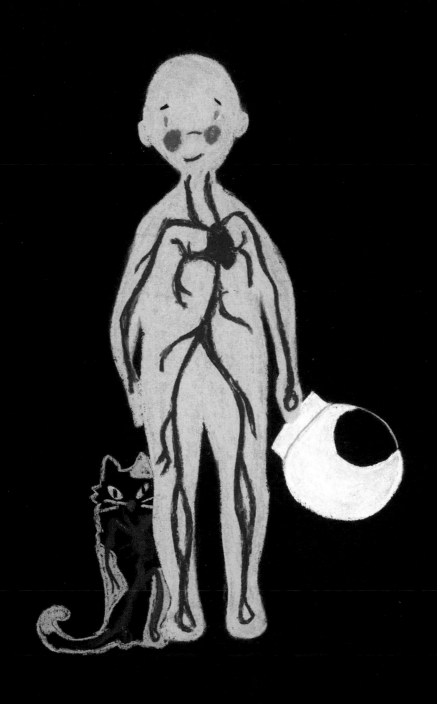

This is an organ, a human eye. You see light with your eyes, and when you look into a mirror, light lets you see your eyes looking back at you.

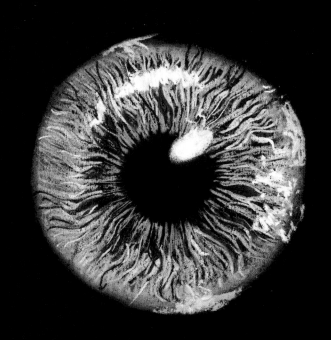

Your youniverse holds many organs. Each organ is made of tissues holding many blood cells and many, many molecules with many, many, many atoms.

Your body is holding this book, which is made from trees, which are made from tissues, which are made from cells, which are made from molecules, which are made from atoms that are almost impossibly tiny yet have built the universe and your youniverse.

You can hold this book because the electron clouds in your fingers push back against the electron clouds in the book.

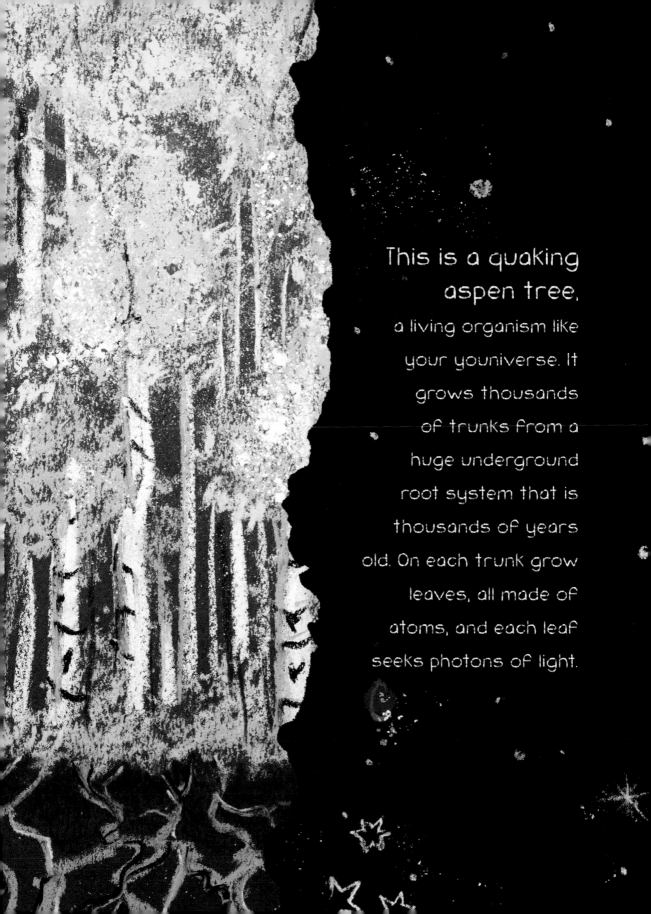

This is a quaking aspen tree, a living organism like your youniverse. It grows thousands of trunks from a huge underground root system that is thousands of years old. On each trunk grow leaves, all made of atoms, and each leaf seeks photons of light.

These are leaves.
They are green because
they contain a pigment
called chlorophyll.

A leaf uses molecules
of chlorophyll to
harvest photons of light
and produce oxygen
molecules that your
youniverse breathes.

Creeping fig vine

In a rainbow, light traveling through water droplets is refracted into seven wavelengths of color. Red is the longest wavelength. Blue is the shortest. Billions of droplets with trillions of molecules and many trillions of atoms sculpt photons into this arc of colors across the sky.

Light can be squashed or stretched as it streaks through the universe. Some light is stretched so far it becomes invisible to our eyes.

*African
red-knobbed sea star*

All of us reading this book, and every human not reading this book, live on a planetary body called Earth. Our one Earth is home to many rainbows and billions of people who have trillions of blood cells, each with millions of molecules and many millions of atoms.

Our Earth is mostly blue because light from the sun is scattered in the sky and reflected from the water in oceans and rivers pooled around the globe.

This is a beam of sunlight streaming
trillions of photons per second to Earth.

If we follow it a little more than eight minutes
into the past, we will arrive at our sun.

The sun is a star, a nuclear
factory where photons are birthed.
Our star shines light and warmth,
gifting Earth with life.

It holds many, many, many trillions
of atoms, though it is too hot for
molecules to survive for long.

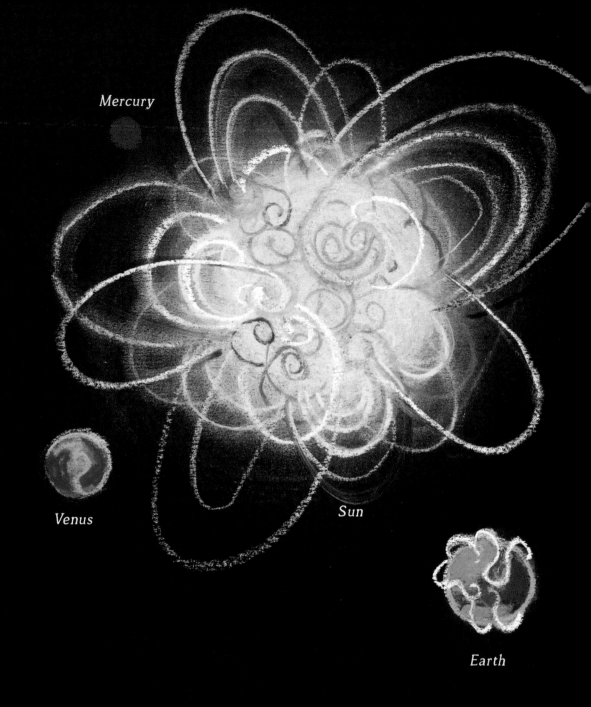

Mercury

Venus

Sun

Earth

This is our solar system, our town in the galaxy.
It holds many planetary bodies and our one sun.

Mars

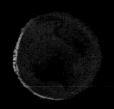

Uranus

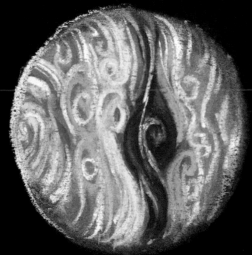

Neptune is the
most distant known
planet in our solar
system—the last
big building on the
edge of town.

Jupiter

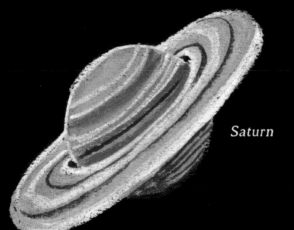

Saturn

Neptune

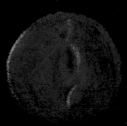

If you could visit Neptune and look back toward Earth with a telescope, you would see a tiny pale-blue dot in the distance—our home.

Beyond Neptune are the outskirts of town—Pluto and other icy objects, perhaps even another planet, not yet discovered, orbiting darkly billions of miles away, like an unlit building in the night.

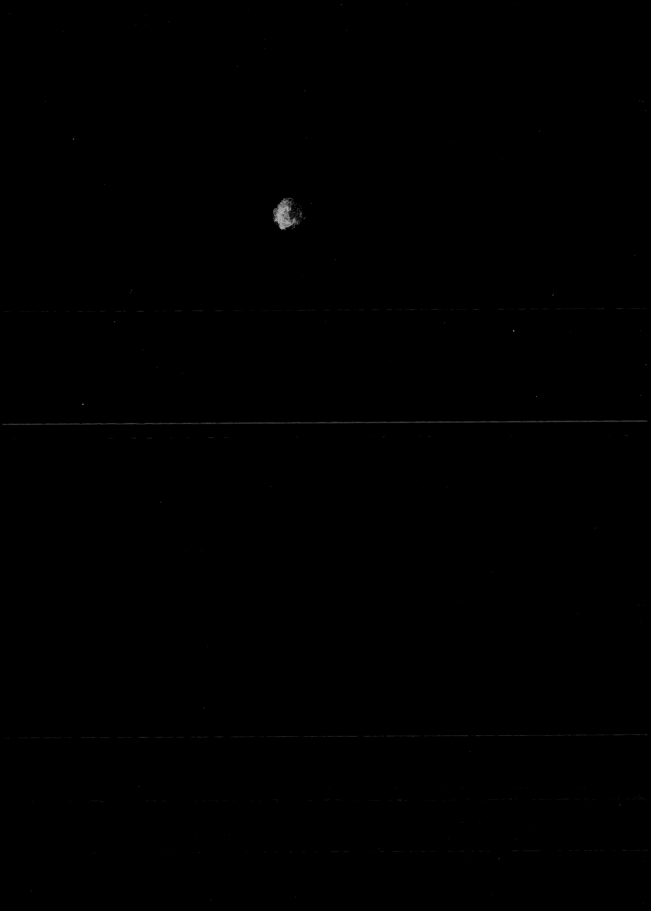

You are here.

This is our galaxy, the Milky Way. It holds our solar system and many, many, many other stars, perhaps hundreds of billions of them. Most of them have planetary bodies.

A pulse of light reaches us from the sun in just over eight minutes but would take 100,000 years to cross the Milky Way. Our solar system is orbiting around the center of the Milky Way at 490,000 miles per hour (220 kilometers per second), and the Milky Way galaxy is hurtling through space at more than a million miles per hour (450 kilometers per second).

This is the Butterfly Nebula,
a cloud of dust and gas flung
outward by a dying star. It takes
3,800 years for light to reach us
from this cloud in our galaxy.

In a nebula, matter and energy can be recycled into new stars, new factories for atoms, fusing elements to create more building blocks for planets and living things.

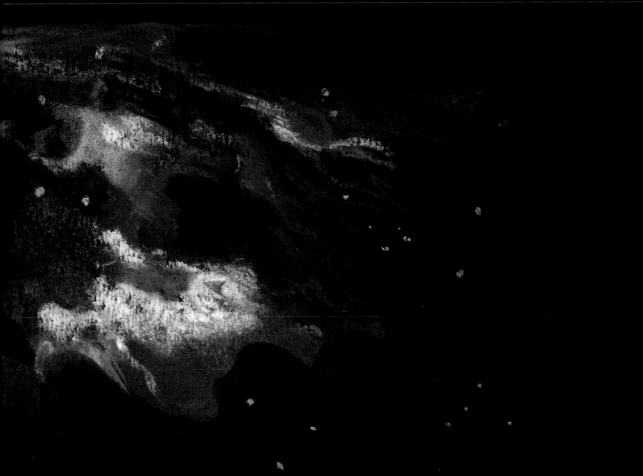

Smiling at us through the vast expanse of space beyond the Milky Way is the Cheshire Cat galaxy group. It is a cluster of galaxies visible through a powerful telescope. The light we see started its journey to our eyes before Earth was born 4.6 billion years ago.

This is space, everything you see and everything you can't see. It holds many, many, many gazillions of molecules and many, many, many, many gazillions of atoms.

Space and time are laced together into a fabric called space-time, which supports everything you see and everything you can't see in its palm.

The oldest light started its voyage
through space-time more than 13 billion years
ago. You can't see it, but cosmologists can hear
it. This light has been stretched into microwave
radiation, and its static echoes through space.

Stars are born, blaze brightly, burn out, and launch atoms into space. Atoms of the universe became the atoms of your youniverse. You are made of stars.

Leaves, flowers, streams, cats, cities, and your home travel with you on this beautiful blue planetary body we call Earth.

You and they fly thousands of miles through space in the time it takes to read this sentence. Their atoms, like your atoms, were forged in stars.

Atoms with their electron clouds have given you the ability to read these words and think about what you're reading. They have created your extraordinary imagination, a spark of light in the universe. And they have created another kind of consciousness in the quaking aspen, a spark we do not yet fully understand.

The leaf, the flower, the stream, the cat, the quaking aspen, and your home are visible in your imagination even when you can't see them. Each one is a miracle, and your imagination is the greatest of miracles, a mind that contemplates the atoms and the stars from which it is made.

Even the vast empty spaces
of the universe are not empty,
because your imagination fills them.

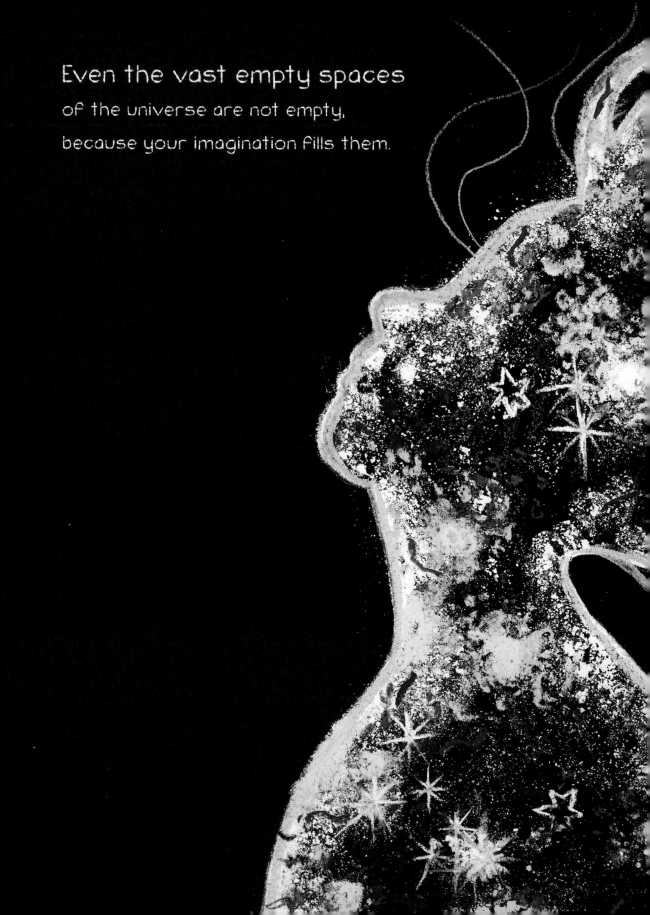

Your imagination radiates
outward, faster than light,
and can travel anywhere.

This is you,
gazing
into the
universe.

This is the
YOUNIVERSE.

To every particle that formed this book
and to Kenji, my inspiration, thank you.
—Liz

© 2022 by Lizelle van der Merwe

Hardcover ISBN 978-0-88448-955-9

Library of Congress Control Number 2022940576

10 9 8 7 6 5 4 3 2 1

All rights reserved. No part of this publication may be reproduced
or transmitted in any form or by any means, electronic or mechani-
cal, including photocopying, recording, or any information storage or
retrieval system, without permission in writing from the publisher.

Tilbury House Publishers

Thomaston, Maine

www.tilburyhouse.com

Designed by Frame25 Productions

Printed in China on FSC®-certified paper

FSC
www.fsc.org

MIX

Paper | Supporting
responsible forestry

FSC® C013314